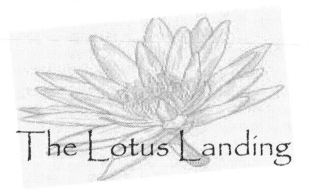

The Lotus Landing

THE LOTUS LANDING
QUOTES ON TRUTH AND TRANSCENDENCE

iUniverse books may be ordered through booksellers or by contacting:

iUniverse
1663 Liberty Drive
Bloomington, IN 47403
www.iuniverse.com
1-800-Authors (1-800-288-4677)

ISBN: 978-1-5320-8815-5 (sc)
ISBN: 978-1-5320-8816-2 (e)

Library of Congress Control Number: 2019918150

Print information available on the last page.

iUniverse rev. date: 12/04/2019

The Lotus Landing:

Quotes on Truth and Transcendence

By: Sherrie L. Engram

About the Author

Sherrie L. Engram is a noted poet and author. She resides in Florida, where she continues her passion for writing and literary pursuits.

For more information about Sherrie L. Engram visit her website at www.sherrielengram.com.

More Works by Sherrie L. Engram

Until My Heart's Content: Poems on Love, Loss, and Life

Quotes From Under An Oak: Quotes on Love, Loss, and Life

Dedication

I dedicate this book to those who seek out
Wisdom, Truth, and Justice, in all that
they encounter, and utilize that knowledge
for the betterment of this Earth.

I also dedicate this book to my
wonderful mother Roselin, who I am
eternally grateful and blessed to have as a
loving, insightful, and caring mother and
who has nurtured and instilled in me
the love of The Arts and Sciences.

Enlightenment comes as a flash of lightning
when we are standing as still as a rod.

-Sherrie L. Engram

Table of Contents

Foreword

As I travel and gain perspective of the world, my exploration into the Human Condition continues. The penning of *The Lotus Landing*, is a further inspection into the Human Experience.

This book takes on a new vantage point of thought, in a sense that, it gathers more inquisition than it attempts to answer. The lotus flower has many meanings throughout both modern and ancient cultures, but the essence of what it symbolizes are Rebirth, Truth, and Enlightenment. The imagery of a radiant flower blooming atop a murky abyss clean, pristine, and renewed, gives inspiration to even the most pedestrian of individuals. This insightful collection of original quotes and aphorisms is an extended examination into the realm of our existence and touches on philosophical ideals, Human Nature, Reason, and Faith.

Love, Life, & Death

The flavors in the
Elixir of Life are all the same.
Open the chalice of your mind and
share your philosophies, passions, and
your pains so that we may all drink
and commune together in this world.

Surrender to a higher power, for
that is the key to Life itself.
Relinquish yourself to the Universe
and find your purpose in the process.

Life on earth is an affair.
One, that you do not choose, but one, that
you cannot possibly help but to plan and
dream of adventurous and extravagant
rendezvous with Destiny.

You can spend a lifetime
obsessing over possessions,
engulfed in vanity and sexuality,
and consumed by
both money and conformity,
but would that be much of a life?

A path that is forged through
fire, brimstone, and brawn cannot be
constructed in a linear fashion.

True love can be a mirror into
our souls, but for some it is better to
only glance at the prospect
of it, than to attain it.

The Grave, is merely a
quaint and quiet bed
for eternal sleepers.

Falling in love with yourself
happens more than only once in a lifetime.

Search your soul for love and
if you can love yourself, then it should
not be so hard for others to do the same.

From Death there must be Birth
to give the Cycle of Life its worth.

Our perception of Death
is our litmus test for our
purpose of Life.

To solve the mystery of Life,
start by living yours to the
fullest of your potential
then believe in God
to take you even higher.

Oftentimes keeping a sound mind
is the heaviest burden
we may bear in our lifetime.

Love is very complex and its complexity leads to its complications and notoriety.

Your Cupola of Life is either
overflowing or underfilled.

Live, Speak, and Commune
with the living, do not seek out
the dead and disturb their slumber.

There are no second chances at Life, there are only those who got away from the Reaper and those whom have ran into his hearse.

Life is a game we all play,
but some sit at the High Rollers tables
while others stand and watch.

What of Love?
What of Truth and Beauty?
If there is no acknowledgment
of their omnipotent power?

In Life, no one wakes up to a
Winter morning, without first
witnessing the birth of Spring,
the blistering sun of Summer,
and the falling leaves of Autumn,
so too, is the oscillating journey of Life.

Only in Death,
do we find regard and meaning
for Life and the life thereafter.

The simple things give
Life its comedy and grit.

If you have no respect for Life, then why should you be so keen on the afterlife?

Love is both respect and acceptance, and
without the two there is only consumption.

Your life to date,
is made up of
all the choices you have made
from the day you began to take hold
and accountability of your life.

True Love is worth the quest.

To sit still,
and not think of all the things
you are missing
because you are sitting still,
is the Secret of Life.

True Love, is not fully comprehending why you love someone, yet you fully comprehend every aspect of the person even before you have met them.

There is no other way out of life
than to live through each moment of it
with the best of your abilities.

The Comedy of Life is that
you only get a good seat
to watch it unfold when you're dead.

I found my true love,
and was repulsed
because he reminded me
too much of myself.

Would there be a question of Life
if Death were not so pertinent
in our minds?

Realize that one is lonesome,
but two come together to make one,
yet never live life as just one.

True Love,
is not knowing exactly why
you love so strongly for another, yet
you know without a doubt
you do indeed love!

Most people are laissez-faire about Life
and
make a large commotion over Death.

Do not attend your life, but attain it through enlightenment and prayer.

Nature & Man

Wisdom is never given,
it is discovered through the railways
and passages of where our life takes us.
It is a perspective unique to us but a
journey that is universal among men.

Make yourself like the mycorrhizea
humble and low to the trees and your
value will become far above rubies.

The life of Man is effervescent
coming and going as quickly into
the world as a flash of lightning.

Those that escape predation
pass on their genes and stories.

The feet run and carry you
throughout life, so too does,
the woman run and carry life,
but seldom are they both revered
for having such importance.

If the Animal awakens each day
knowing its purpose, then
why cannot Man do the same?

Deep down in the
Well of Human Consciousness,
the desires and fears of every man
are given the same light.

The duality of man
is only a fraction of the other
myriad of characteristics that
makeup an individual.

The other half of my soul is waiting
for me to appear just as anxiously.

Each and every soul has
wisdom and virtue embedded inside, and it
may take a man all his life to search and find it.

How a man rekindles a fireless flame is evident by the glibness of his tongue.

My mind is as fit as an infant
and as wise as an old fish.

If a man is neither bemused
nor irritated by the truth,
then give him lies and bread.

Not all of your faults
can be covered by the veneers
and the facades of your forefathers.

It takes a skilled craftsman
twenty years to learn and perfect
the ingenuity of his craft and only
about twenty minutes for a machine
programmed to do the same technique.
Yet, as time wears on, the artist passes
on his unique talents and skills to
an apprentice for posterity while the
machine merely becomes obsolete.

Even the smallest of mice can
trigger fear in the mighty stallion.

The cankerous wail of a Holler monkey
is music to his lover's ears.

The endurance of
the Human Condition knows no end,
but the wealth of a man can find many ends.

Writers sharpen the intellect and
the blades of the Human Condition.

Why walk on blazed paths when the
uncharted wilderness beckons?

The Lotus,
rises above the muck of the pond, and
shines bright and white while being
nurtured from the dark waters below.

In the woods a deer is a companion
and a delight for the lone traveler, but
a meal and a trophy for the brigade.

Within the trauma and break of the psyche,
do we psychologists not find the essence of
the human condition and ourselves?

Clairvoyance is how the wise man
describes his burden.
Quackery is what the layman
calls his business.

Bamboo is thin and weak, but it is
sufficient for the mighty Panda bear.

We are most often
humble and gracious to others, and
haughty and egregious to ourselves.

If men were lords of themselves there
would be no place and no purpose for God.

The bee merges its proboscis
into the nectar and the nectar
emerges into the bee.

Who can hold on to Vanity?
My once rosy cheeks are now weighed
down by gravity, the space between my
teeth have widened into gaps, and my
nose hangs millimeters lower skewing
the symmetry of my immaculate face.
I cannot cling and holdfast to Vanity,
but through the ages
I hold my mind intact.

The first generation worked,
the second generation invested,
the third generation rested, and
the fourth generation wept.

The act of a predator catching its prey
is a resounding truth that
both know all too well.

Nature has such whims and wiles
that can outpace any poet's quill.

Every man has within himself
uncertainties, doubts, and mysteries;
and in the same respect,
outwardly he can embody
confidence, honor, and humility.

A fruit needs only time
to ripen in and of itself.

Most men are vain from nature
and nurtured into civility.

There is magic in Nature, and
Am I not a part of Nature?

Every animal in nature knows its
purpose in the world except Man.

The reflection in the mirror
is undeniably you, but in
your mind's eye, you are much
more taller and handsome.

Do not distinguish yourself from God,
for He has made you perfectly in
His image and worketh your hands
in everything good and perfect.

Artists in every media
shine a light into the darkened
abyss of the human condition.

Charge with me,
my brothers into the battlefield.
I will answer,
to God alone, for this course of action,
but each man will testify
for their own soul before Him alone.

Mountainous terrain are never smooth and straight, for they are tortuous and dangerous; but nothing can compare to the summit's panoramic views.

The verses of profound poets
cannot outmatch the reverence
and majestic beauty of Nature.

A master writer exposes his mind and vulnerabilities, and in the process unlocks the psyche of humankind.

The discerning eye sees even
the smallest of hairline factures
in the Queen's finest tea cups.

An artist's brush strokes are the
extension of the fibers of his soul.

Your true nature always ripples up from underneath the bog of your character.

When the bridegroom
finds no more amazement in the bride,
then the appearance of a mistress
is only a physical representation
of an already present inward malady.

Nature,
does not have to provide all
the commentary for all of
Life's challenges.

The Great Flood,
fell as droplets of rain one at a time.

Never ask a man a question
that is best suited to be
answered by God.

Both the earth and the minds of the youth
are soft and impressionable; therefore, both
must be nurtured and protected from pollution.

How unlearned are the scholarly, and
how sensible are the animals.

True human nature is revealed
in the trenches of our psyche when
exhaustion, hunger, and doubt
have all reached their peak.

Find the threads that bind you to humankind, and then knot off the ends.

New branches of a tree bared fruit,
and thanked God for the blessing.
Old and dead branches fell to the
ground to nourish the tree, and
thanked God for their new purpose.

Truth & Transcendence

We sit to settle ourselves
on a foundation that is
existential to any room.

Search high and low for your destiny
then seek your dormant soul, give it
a nudge, and live out all of its dreams.

The only role model worth following is Jesus Christ, he was and is perfect in everyway.

You should look for the least resistance.
Never sever what could be untied,
and never break what could be folded.

The burden of Enlightenment
is too heavy for you to hold
on to anything else.

Always question everything, and
in the process you may find an answer.

We are enslaved by our conformity.
Preoccupied with abundance, acceptance, and
affection. We must liberate ourselves from their
codependence and be as free as a stumped tree.

Often in times of hunger and famine water and stale breadcrumbs are a feast of delight, but in times of plenty stale breadcrumbs go unnoticed.

The harlequin wears a mask
of white paint to reflect and reveal
the many masks of Humanity.

Enlightenment is attainable, and it breathes every waking moment, therefore do not suffocate it with fantasy and illusionment.

Take down all of your false idols
because in the end there is but
only one true God; therefore, seek
Him for refuge and guidance.

For questions
search high and low, far and wide,
but for answers search within yourself.

We are all changing involuntarily, and in constant stages of cell replication and decay; but the mind is the same as yesterday, and will be the same tomorrow unless it is actively renewed.

The realm of Enlightenment ignites all
fallacies and falsehoods until
our vanity and illusions are white ash.

The rain from the heavens falls
gently and precisely onto the rose while
the water collected upon the cedar
rooftops falls haphazardly.

In order to be filled with both
peace and understanding
you need to be both receptive and empty.

The Mind and the Cosmos are
intertwined like the cobwebs of
dust and diamond powder in the
studio of a Master Diamond Cutter.

Why search the foothills and
mountaintops for enlightenment?
Enlightenment,
is everywhere and in everything.

The Realm of Awareness has no doors,
and it is paramount that on the
conscious level each individual have
the ability to discern that they are
awakened in every moment.

In order to perfect your character you
must be tested and placed into
the furnace and then tried by fire.

The past is unchangeable,
the present is attainable, and
the future is intangible.

Do not become a mover of motions,
but really contemplate.
Why is movement necessary; and what
will doing so accomplish?

From humility of spirit we gain
honor and more humility.

You may pick up something sizable
once you have dropped what
is already in your hands.

The old and bowed
must wither away
to make room for the
fresh and burgeoning youth.

Your weakness whines and tells you to quit at an inopportune moment, but your character commands you to stay and make the opportunity appear.

The number eight is the luckiest number of them all. Turn it on its side and you will find infinity and beyond.

The upswept winds in the cedar roofs are content to be trapped indoors while the captured wild winds howls and whistles as it makes its daring escape through the cracks.

Stir up your mind, uplift your wings,
stiffen up the sinews, and rattle your bones.
Movement is a conscious decision
although some movements are
involuntary, yet awareness of this
matter of fact is always the resounding key.

What is existence?
What is nonexistence?
What lies between the two?
Are they not two sides of the same coin?

Make your bed upon
vanity and falsehoods, and your dreams
will become your new imprisonment.

Do not travel too far from the self,
for your instincts are keen enough
to notice your neglect.

Do not blame Society
for its delusions, but rather take a stand
and avoid them all together.

Knowledge by seeing is simple; but
knowledge through the excavation of
the unknown and unseen terrain
of the soul is genius.

Awareness of self and time
are two illusions forged into reality
that are sentient in Nature.

Enlightenment,
can become a sickness of the mind
if the spirit is not uplifted
in its attainment.

What we often see in reality,
and what we truly hope will someday
come to pass is somehow only a small
break in the streamline of infinity.

A simple twist of the hand
shows man what is above is similar,
yet still distinct from what is below.

If you obtain every goal of
your lifetime, then you will weep
for the lost of enlightenment.

Lessen the desires of your heart,
and your life will become more focused
on your contribution to the world
rather than your consumption.

If there is nothing to learn or know,
then why do our senses fool us so?

Each day I grow complex,
I also grow vex.
I must strive for simplicity and puerility.

Dream with full fervor and might,
for you can lie idle while awake.

If you are blind to your path,
then you cannot see it
even if, you are blazing the trail.

Are you on the side of the
Angels, Devils, or Truth?

Solitary Peace is a more
copacetic term than death.

A plain mind is merely a beast of the wild while an enlightened mind is tamed by discipline and disillusionment.

We receive
what we place out into the world.
The timid voice receives a gentle echo
while the booming voice an avalanche.

Walk into the unknown, for it is the only way to gain perspective and truth.

The world is yours if you can
construct it from scratch on the page.

Begin each day anew then
begin to live renewed.

To know when one is truly full perhaps one has to know what true emptiness is.

Emptiness on the inside is oftentimes
filled with possessions, obsessions,
and depression on the outside.

Alas, My Friends, if my work here on
Earth, survives me, then it
will be my only link to immortality.

It is hard to stop increasing the dosage of a self diagnosed and self medicated prescription.

The Night somehow uncovers
everyone's secrets.

When you find the place
of enlightenment, then
be courteous and take others with you.

All separation and classism are all
imagined then written down and
then cultivated as truth in our society.

Where are all the unbeaten tracks?
There seems to be guideposts
left by others everywhere.

Meditation is not just a trendy way
to relieve anxiety and stress.
It is a supplication to a higher power
that takes both faith and openness
to receive clarity of the mind
by freeing it over to God.

Viewing things
hidden in plain sight
is often how a wise man views the world.

Possessions have a certain
way of tethering us to them.

Go forth, go forward, and go full force,
but never backwards.

It is better to spend more hours of the day investigating the issues of your heart than the speculation and affairs of others.

A quiet mind free from
distraction, desire, and doubt
is likened to a Nirvana.

It is a blessing to both
be alive and to be able to contribute
to the grand scheme of things.

Seeing yourself in your mind's eye
already enlightened
is akin to meeting your soul halfway.

Listening and waiting for the rain
is always what you are truly after.

The mounting collections of your
prized possessions become either trash,
or under someone else's possession
when you are dead and gone.

The crashing waves of the mind
upwell the deep chasms of the psyche
and release gems of knowledge.

The world of a cosmopolitan
is no larger than
a man with an opened mind.

Charisma,
is the catalyst for your charm,
but your Character,
is anchored and powered by your control.

Seeing and observing,
are two different analytical pathways
of acknowledgement.
You can see most things, but a level of
awareness is needed for true observation.

Switch off the world, sever the
yoke of bondage to technology, and
disrobe your vanity. These are the first
steps to finding your true self.

Your time is your treasure, so guard it with the upmost care, and do not tarry and squander your greatest inheritance.

Possessions are pirates that ransom our time, our energy, and our money.

Reality, will make any man a believer
in anything other than True Reality.

Eyes of Blue, Green, or Brown
can only see themselves in the
reflection of another's eyes.

Do not be deluded by yourself, for
there are many others who will
offer to do that freely for you.

The proverbial Paradise has never
been lost, just merely,
misplaced, mislabeled, and misjudged.

Each possession stakes a claim on us.

The Ends of the Earth, are only
what you perceive the end to be.

Be careful of pointing fingers
and always be aware of which finger
is pointing to you.

Open your eyes
to the joys and laughter of Life
so that you may encounter
every moment of the ecstasy of living.

Lose yourself and become like
the looking glass, and you will
undoubtedly see everything you are
and are not in the eyes of others.

If you limit the World,
to only what your eyes can see and
your hands can touch, then by your
own definition you are limited indeed.

When you are gasping for breath it is,
then that you find the time to search
within yourself for the resolve
needed for the next breath.

Do not become a tourist of the world; but
rather dive in, make roots, or build something.

The truth has a funny way of making
all the miseries of life very funny.

The truth is always present, for it
makes its own entrance and exit wounds.

Pillars and pedestals are not needed
in the sanctuary of the mind.

The things of this world are redundant.
The fashion, technology, and money
are all recycled and never fully go away.

Be present in this era.
Be alive, smile, and sing, for you will
never have this moment arrive again.

You can hear of the unique blessings
and you may even see them manifest;
but only when you have experienced
God, then and only then can you
truly know for yourself.

Holding back your true intentions
leads to roads off of your charted
course, and more detours on
your way back to the source.

When you are down
on both knees begging God for
supplication and forgiveness it is,
then that He is right beside you
trying to lift you to your feet.

Is there no end to suffering, and
must the future always bring more?

Looking at a problem and its many
effects is much more easier than
understanding and discovering its main cause.

Let go of the physical and
grasp the metaphysical instead.

Keep your mind calm, collected,
and sharp; and it will never
hold on to insanity, delusion,
or sugarcoated rhetoric.

Shine your light inwardly and
it cannot help but to glow outwardly.

Your beliefs are semi-truths
that need only an accomplice and
time to become the real thing.

Without refinement of both
mind and spirit my other half
would seldom recognize me.

To be in the presence of greatness
is not the same as attaining it,
just as seeing a shooting star is
not the same as grasping it.

Our morality gives us an excuse
for the fragility of our
convictions and character.

If you would like to build a house,
then simply build it. Nothing gets done
until you take up your hands.

In the mind there are no shores left unchartered and no mountain too great that it cannot be conquered.

Enlightenment
comes as a flash of lightning when
we are standing as still as a rod.

Adaptation is the key to survival, but
amiability is the key to everything else.

Your dreams are much more realized and
obtained when you are awakened in the mind.

Give your best and then seek the
Lord to discover your very best.

What is an actual universal absolute
and can we ever truly find one, or merely
go about finding the ways and the means
in which to completely justify one?

Pedestrian individuals are merely mundane people who are conscious of the world, but have never been quite conscious of the wonderful and exciting role they each play within it.

Reaching the state of enlightenment to further your exploration of the world is futile if the knowledge is not shared.

Our hopes often gives us the resolve
for life's challenges while our obstacles
often makes us all practitioners of patience.

If you reach only for fact,
then you will undoubtedly
formulate sound reason.

While on the journey of finding your true destiny you may oftentimes help others find theirs also along the way.

Begin anew each day and
then reset the gears of the
churning master clock to your race.

In the Realm of the Mind,
reaching the state of absolute Solitary Peace,
is also absolute freedom from the world.

To freely breathe in and out
on one's own is a cherished gift
too commonplaced to be treasured.

A singular unique vision and expert pioneering can pave a path on this earth that others may choose to follow, but your deeds also carve a Tablet of Truth, that you alone will recite in heaven.

The Sword of Truth will always
prevail, for everything in darkness
comes into its light.

A mind that functions both clearly
and independently is a space of
profound reverence and renaissance.

There is ultimately a supreme difference
between both the sacred and the secular, and
thus in order to find it, you must seek the Divine.

The mind is an intricate and flawless pearl,
and the more it is nurtured with the nacre
of Truth, Wisdom, and Reason
the more luster it will attain.

Explaining all the details of the
vast intricacies and complexities of the
grand scale universe takes all the
joy and wonderment out of continued
Space Exploration because
mystery can be as fetching as a mistress.

Stir up the waves within your idle and aqueous soul, and then cast your future's net wide and long to catch your ordained destiny.

In the Realm of Enlightenment,
there are multiple entrances and only
one main exit by way of illusionment.

If you look into only the things you can
see and touch, then you will only begin
to scratch the surface of the tangible; but
rather try searching within your soul for the
intangible and somehow you will meet
God in the middle.

How could this world be both perfect and
have everlasting peace? Where then in the
Realm of the Cosmos would Heaven belong?

Perhaps it is too often that we seek
that in which we may lack and never fully
utilize that in which we may already possess.

What if there was nothing else to garner from
the immense universe?
What if gaining knowledge was just a
rudimentary pratice?
What if all of the human condition could
somehow be absorbed by osmosis of the mind?
What then, would we probe and quest for
on this earth?

Silence, is both an inaudible and ominous gatekeeper and thus in order to gain entrance into the unknown, you must do so quietly.

The quintessential performing art form
of sequential and rhythmic movement
set to both meter and rhyme.
Dance! Joyous Dance!
Truly and undeniably dance
is living and breathing art in motion.

Art reflects Life so that mankind
may look itself thoroughly in the eyes
even when it has been blinded.

Our ulimate choice in life is absolutely crystal
clear, either sleep in the pilant and complacent
Bed of Illusionment or be awakened into the
Realm of Enlightenment with the urgent speed
of the realization of the supreme need for God.

We know so much, yet there still
remains an unquenchable thirst,
insatiable desire, and herculean effort
to set one's cap for the unknowable.

Printed in the United States
By Bookmasters